BULLRING TECHNO MAKEOUT JAMZ

by Nathan Queeley-Dennis

‖ SAMUEL FRENCH ‖

FOR AMATEUR PRODUCTION ENQUIRIES

UNITED KINGDOM AND WORLD
EXCLUDING NORTH AMERICA
licensing@concordtheatricals.co.uk
020-7054-7298

Each title is subject to availability from Concord Theatricals, depending upon country of performance.

---

known or yet to be invented, including mechanical, electronic, digital, photocopying, recording, videotaping, or otherwise, without the prior written permission of the publisher. No one shall share this title, or part of this title, to any social media or file hosting websites.

The moral right of Nathan Queeley-Dennis to be identified as author of this work has been asserted in accordance with Section 77 of the Copyright, Designs and Patents Act 1988.

USE OF COPYRIGHTED MUSIC

A licence issued by Concord Theatricals to perform this play does not include permission to use the incidental music specified in this publication. In the United Kingdom: Where the place of performance is already licensed by the PERFORMING RIGHT SOCIETY (PRS) a return of the music used must be made to them. If the place of performance is not so licensed then application should be made to PRS for Music (www.prsformusic.com). A separate and additional licence from PHONOGRAPHIC PERFORMANCE LTD (www.ppluk.com) may be needed whenever commercial recordings are used. Outside the United Kingdom: Please contact the appropriate music licensing authority in your territory for the rights to any incidental music.

USE OF COPYRIGHTED THIRD-PARTY MATERIALS

Licensees are solely responsible for obtaining formal written permission from copyright owners to use copyrighted third-party materials (e.g., artworks, logos) in the performance of this play and are strongly cautioned to do so. If no such permission is obtained by the licensee, then the licensee must use only original materials that the licensee owns and controls. Licensees are solely responsible and liable for clearances of all third-party copyrighted materials, and shall indemnify the copyright owners of the play(s) and their licensing agent, Concord Theatricals Ltd., against any costs, expenses, losses and liabilities arising from the use of such copyrighted third-party materials by licensees.

IMPORTANT BILLING AND CREDIT REQUIREMENTS

If you have obtained performance rights to this title, please refer to your licensing agreement for important billing and credit requirements.

BULLRING TECHNO MAKEOUT JAMZ was first produced by Ellie Keel for Ellie Keel Productions in Paines Plough's Roundabout at the Edinburgh Festival Fringe in August 2023. The play was part of Ellie Keel's *Fearlessly Imaginative // Endlessly Exciting* Summer Season. It was an Ellie Keel Productions, Paines Plough, and Belgrade Theatre co-production, in association with the Royal Exchange Theatre. The cast was as follows:

NATHANIEL................................Nathan Queeley-Dennis

CREATIVE TEAM

Writer | Nathan Queeley-Dennis

Director | Dermot Daly

Designer | Caitlin Mawhinney

Lighting Designer | David Doyle

Composer & Sound Designer | Tom Foskett-Barnes

Company Stage Manager | Aime Neeme

Dramaturgy | Dermot Daly, Suzanne Bell, and Tommo Fowler

Founded in 2019, Ellie Keel Productions (EKP) specialises in producing fearlessly imaginative new plays by outstanding writers and creative teams. Previous EKP productions include the multi-award-winning *SAP* by Rafaella Marcus (Roundabout, followed by Soho Theatre and national tour), *Collapsible* by Margaret Perry (HighTide Festival at Assembly, then Dublin's Abbey Theatre Dublin and Bush Theatre), and *HOTTER* by Mary Higgins and Ell Potter (Underbelly, 2019, then Soho Theatre and national tour). Ellie Keel's other credits include *The Swell* by Isley Lynn (Orange Tree Theatre, London), *You Bury Me* by Ahlam (Bristol Old Vic, Royal Lyceum Theatre, Edinburgh, and Orange Tree Theatre, London), *Reasons You Should(n't) Love Me* by Amy Trigg (Kiln Theatre and national tour), *Still No Idea* by Lisa Hammond and Rachael Spence (Traverse Theatre, Southbank Centre and tour), *FITTER* by Mary Higgins and Ell Potter (Soho Theatre), and *Redefining Juliet* (Barbican). Ellie Keel is the Founder Director of the Women's Prize for Playwriting.

**Paines
Plough**

Paines Plough is the national theatre of new plays. A touring company dedicated entirely to developing and producing exceptional new writing, the work we create connects with artists and communities across the UK.

"The lifeblood of the UK's theatre ecosystem." – The Guardian

Since 1974 Paines Plough has worked with over 300 world renowned playwrights including James Graham, Sarah Kane, Dennis Kelly, Kae Tempest, Vinay Patel, Mike Bartlett, Sam Steiner, Elinor Cook, and Zia Ahmed.

Our plays are nationally identified and locally heard. We tour to over 40 places a year and are committed to bringing work to communities who might not otherwise have the opportunity to experience much new writing or theatre. We reach over 30,000 people annually from Cornwall to the Orkney Islands, in village halls, off-Broadway, and in our own pop-up theatre Roundabout; a state of the art, in the round auditorium which travels the length and breadth of the country.

"That noble company Paines Plough, de facto national theatre of new writing." – The Telegraph

Furthering our reach beyond theatre walls, our audio app Come to Where I'm From hosts 180 original mini plays about home and our digital projects connect with audiences via WhatsApp, phone, email, and even by post.

Wherever you are, you can experience a Paines Plough production.

"I think some theatre just saved my life." – @kate_clement on Twitter

BELGRADE THEATRE
COVENTRY

The Belgrade is Coventry's largest professional theatre, producing and presenting a diverse range of shows, events, and ground-breaking community and education initiatives. In its landmark building, across the region, the UK, and online, it uses theatre to entertain, inspire, share the city's stories, uncover hidden histories, and unleash the creativity of diverse communities.

64 years ago, critic Kenneth Tynan saw the theatre's completion as the beginning of a new era. "Enter most theatres and it's the gilded, cupidaceous past," he wrote. "Enter this one, and you enter the future." The theatre is now 18 months into a new future, led by CEO Laura Elliot and Creative Director Corey Campbell. These leaders have ambitious plans to build on the Theatre"s rich history of pioneering theatre, participation, and talent development – to realise a lasting place of sanctuary for creatives and communities.

Through values of **COLLABORATION**, **EVOLUTION**, and **AUTHENTICITY**, their working mission is to **USE THE TRANSFORMATIVE POWER OF THEATRE TO ENRICH THE PEOPLE OF COVENTRY** and **BEYOND**.

Over the next three years, they will lead a people first approach; prioritising co-creation and cultural democracy; aiming to be a leading example of a regional inclusive learning theatre that sits at the heart of its community.

EXECUTIVE AND SENIOR MANAGEMENT TEAM

CEO | Laura Elliot

Creative Director | Corey Campbell

Director of Finance | Neil Harris

General Manager | Vera Ding

Head of Development | Helen Hotchkiss

Director of Production & Operations | Adrian Sweeney

Head of Communications | Ray Clenshaw

Manchester's Royal Exchange Theatre Company transforms the way people see theatre, each other, and the world around them. Our historic building was taken over by artists in 1976. Today it is an award-winning cultural charity that produces new theatre in-the-round, in communities, on the road, and online.

Exchange remains at the heart of everything we make and do. Now our currency is brand new drama and reinvigorated classics, the boldest artists and a company of highly skilled makers – all brought together in a shared imaginative endeavour to trade ideas and experiences with the people of Greater Manchester (and beyond).

The Exchange's unique auditorium is powerfully democratic, a space where audiences and performers meet as equals, entering and exiting through the same doors. It is the inspiration for all we do; inviting everyone to understand the past, engage in today's big questions, collectively imagine a better future, and lose themselves in the moment of a great night out.

The Royal Exchange was named Regional Theatre of the Year in 2016 and School of the Year at The Stage Awards 2018. Our work, developed with an incredible array of artists and theatre makers, includes *Hamlet* with Maxine Peake (for stage and film), *The Skriker* (with the Manchester International Festival), *King Lear* (co-produced with Talawa Theatre Company, filmed for BBC iPlayer and BBC Four), *The House of Bernarda Alba* (a co-production with Graeae), *Light Falls* (a world-premiere from Simon Stephens directed by Sarah Frankcom with original music by Jarvis Cocker), *Wuthering Heights* (directed by Joint Artistic Director Bryony Shanahan), *Rockets and Blue Lights* (by award-winning writer Winsome Pinnock and directed by Miranda Cromwell), *Cat on a Hot Tin Roof, The Mountaintop* (Digital Streaming directed by Joint Artistic Director Roy Alexander Weise), *All I Want For Christmas* (digital commission for December 2020), *Bloody Elle – A Gig Musical*, and *Let The Right One In* (directed by Bryony Shanahan).

Find out more on our website and social media channels
royalexchange.co.uk
@rxtheatre

The Bruntwood

Prize for Playwriting 2022

in partnership with the **Royal Exchange Theatre**

A partnership between the Royal Exchange Theatre and property company Bruntwood, the Prize is an opportunity for writers of any background and experience to enter unperformed plays for the chance to win part of a prize fund totalling £40,000.

At the heart of the Bruntwood Prize for Playwriting is the principle that anyone and everyone can enter – it is entirely anonymous and scripts are judged purely on the basis of the work alone, with no knowledge of the identity of the playwright. Since its inception in 2005, over 15,000 scripts have been entered, £304,000 has been awarded to 34 prize winning writers, and 26 winning productions have been staged in 38 UK-wide venues.

Each winner enters into a development process with the Royal Exchange Theatre in an endeavour to bring their work to production. It is not guaranteed but we aspire to produce each play and find co-producers to give the plays a longer life and further reach. There have been co-productions with Lyric Hammersmith, Live Theatre, Soho Theatre, Bush Theatre, Orange Tree Theatre, Sherman Theatre, High Tide, and the Royal Court Theatre. Work has also gone on to be produced internationally from Australia, USA, Germany, France, to Canada and Sweden. The Bruntwood Prize International Award was launched in 2019 and, through partnerships with theatres and organisations in Australia, Canada, and the US, accepts submissions from playwrights.

The Bruntwood Prize for Playwriting is a genuine endeavour to discover new stories and help playwrights develop their craft, providing everybody and anybody with the opportunity to write a play. It offers a fantastic opportunity to hone your writing skills, whether or not you have written for the stage before.

More information can be found at www.writeaplay.co.uk

CREATIVE TEAM

NATHAN QUEELEY-DENNIS | WRITER AND PERFORMER

Nathan is an actor and writer from Birmingham. Acting credits include *As You Like It* (@sohoplace); *Black Love* (Kiln Theatre/tiata fahodzi); *A Taste of Honey* (National Theatre); *Really Big and Really Loud* (Paines Plough); *Little Baby Jesus* (Birmingham REP); *Rebel Music* (Middle Child); *Pinocchio* (Orange Tree Theatre); *The War Inside* (VAULT Festival/The Albany); *Girls Like That* (Birmingham REP; World Premiere); *Mittwoch Aus Licht* (Birmingham Opera Company; World Premiere) *Les Misérables in Concert: The 25th Anniversary* (Cameron Mackintosh Ltd) and *Doctors* (BBC).

As a writer he is the overall winner of the Bruntwood Prize for Playwriting 2022 with his debut play *Bullring Techno Makeout Jamz* and is currently working on various projects for Theatre, TV, and Film.

DERMOT DALY | DIRECTOR

Recent directorial credits include: *My Voice Was Heard But It Was Ignored* (Red Ladder Theatre Company; Black British Theatre Awards 2022 winner; Lustrum Winner 2022), *At What A Price* (Leeds Playhouse/British Library), *Aaliyah (after Antigone)* (Freedom Studios), *Kafka's Dick* (Naked Productions/BBC Radio 3), *Initiation* (Audible/LAMDA), *Rise* (Naked Productions/BBC Radio 4).

Dermot has read for the Bruntwood Prize for Playwriting, The Alfred Fagon Award (also as a member of the Jury from 2022), The Mustapha Matura Award, Women's Prize for Playwriting, and Theatre Uncut Political Playwriting Award.

Dermot is a Creative Associate of the Geraldine Connor Foundation, Associate Artist of Arts at the Arms, and has been the (Associate) Artistic director of Freedom Studios. He currently, proudly, serves on the boards of One Tenth Human, Mikron Theatre Company, and Wrongsemble.

CAITLIN MAWHINNEY | DESIGNER

Caitlin was double nominated for Best Designer at The Stage Debut Awards 2022 and awarded the Evening Standard Future Theatre Fund for Visual Design in 2021. She was recently a Creative Associate at Jermyn Street Theatre and a Resident Designer at New Diorama Broadgate.

Caitlin's work has seen main stages and un-conventional spaces across the country.

Recent credits as Set/Costume Designer include: *Dream School* (The Space), *The Island of The Sun* (National Theatre Public Acts, Sunderland

Culture), *The Cyclops* (National Theatre Public Acts, CAST), *Acid's Reign* (Relish Theatre Co.), *The Children's Country House* (Co-design/ Sudbury Hall, National Trust), *Ladies Unleashed, Teechers Leavers '22* (Hull Truck Theatre), *The Anarchist* (Jermyn Street Theatre), *Shake The City, The Sh*t* (Leeds Playhouse/UK Tour), *My Voice Was Heard But It Was Ignored* (Red Ladder Theatre Co./UK Tour), *My Old Man, Is Anyone There?* (imagine if Theatre Co.), *Frisky And Mannish: Popcorn* (Lawrence Batley Theatre), *Our Gate* (Harrogate Theatre)

DAVID DOYLE | LIGHTING DESIGN

David is a multi-award-winning lighting designer working across the UK and Ireland as well as internationally. His work has been seen in Ireland, the UK, The Netherlands, France, Czechia, Switzerland, the USA, and Australia. He was nominated for an Offie for Best Lighting Design for *EAST* at the Kings Head Theatre. Other recent credits include *SAP*, *Outlying Islands* (Atticist), *We Were Promised Honey* (YESYESNONO), *Carmen* (Kings Head Theatre), *Confirmation* (Xnthony), and *The Cat's Mother* (Wildcard). David also works as a producer and is the Executive Producer for Jermyn Street Theatre. www.davidmjtdoyle.com.

TOM FOSKETT-BARNES | COMPOSER & SOUND DESIGN

Tom Foskett-Barnes is a composer and sound designer working predominantly across film, theatre, and sound art. Film credits include Academy Award-nominated documentary *BLACK SHEEP* and BAFTA-nominated short *TONI_WITH_AN_I*. Theatre credits include *SAP* (Roundabout/UK Tour), *WORK.TXT* (Soho Theatre/Staatstheater Mainz), *ANNA BELLA EEMA* (Arcola Theatre), *HOTTER/FITTER* (Soho Theatre) and *THE BEAT OF OUR HEARTS* (Exeter Northcott).

In 2016 Tom was Sound and Music Composer in Residence with ROLI as part of the Embedded_Innovate Scheme and in 2017 Tom was selected as part of the Old Vic 12. Tom trained at the Royal College of Music as a Soirée d'Or Scholar generously supported by a Clifton Parker Award and was the recipient of a BAFTA UK Scholarship.

AIME NEEME | COMPANY STAGE MANAGER

Aime is an Australian stage manager and theatre maker, who likes long walks on the beach, deep chats over a chilled glass of rosé, and whirlwind romances. When she's not looking for love and her house keys, she's travelling around the UK working on the best new writing. Past credits include; *Hungry, Black Love, May Queen, Really Big and Really Loud* (Roundabout Summer Tour 2021), *How to Save the Planet When You're a Young Carer and Broke, Parakeet* (Boundless Theatre), *Dennis of Penge* (Ovalhouse).

CHARACTER

NATHANIEL – He/Him, Black Male from Birmingham of Caribbean descent, twenty-something years old.

SETTING

Birmingham, Brum, 0121, The Second City, Brummagem.

TIME

Is a social construct. *Bullring Techno Makeout Jamz* doesn't exist in a specific time, it's a nostalgic but timeless place.

WRITER'S NOTE

The first question I usually get asked and I get it a lot is if *Bullring Techno Makeout Jamz* is an autobiographical story. It's not at all, although it doesn't help that the character is called Nathaniel, so I sort of brought that on myself. I just named him Nathaniel as a placeholder but then I never changed it.

Although the story is not autobiographical, I always say the feelings and emotions within the play are. My journey with *Bullring Techno Makeout Jamz* is a long one. It started in 2018 as a three-minute monologue way before it even crossed my mind to start developing it into a full play.

I believe the industry ignores Birmingham and the Midlands. I very rarely see plays, TV shows, and films where people sound like me and the people around me growing up unless they're one character of many that's the butt of the jokes. So, I began developing the monologue into a play and it was from a place of frustration.

What stemmed from that was really therapeutic, it eventually became a creative release for me. Five years sounds like a long time, but I'd look at it for thirty minutes then not go back to it again for up to nine months. I'd revisit it in moments where I felt lost, confused, hurt, or angry and it really helped me. As I matured as a person throughout the writing process, I think the story and character matured, or I could just see the story and character way clearer, I've not figured that part out yet.

I'm really glad it came to light the way it did, I never knew how it was going to end when I started, and I don't think it would be the play we have right now if I finished it three or four years ago. It's that idea that everything happens for a reason.

Winning the Bruntwood Prize for Playwriting 2022 was life-changing and I'm so grateful to be in the position I'm in. If you do decide to do this play as a professional production, for drama school auditions, amateur productions etc., just have as much fun as I did writing it, there aren't any rules and theatre is way better when you break its traditional form so please carry that with you.

Bullring Techno Makeout Jamz is an amalgamation of all my fears, anger, frustration, joy, friendships, and failures from my first ten years of life as an adult. All those aspects are sewn into the DNA of the play but ultimately the play is about love. Platonic, Romantic and Self Love.

It's always about love.

NQD.

ACKNOWLEDGEMENTS

Due to the creative process a lot of people have had an impact on myself and *Bullring Techno Makeout Jamz*. Firstly all of the love in the world to my family, my Mom, Dad, Nan, my Brother Marvin and my Auntie Maria who is probably the biggest factor as to why I even work in theatre today.

Producer Jade Samuels and her work for TriForce Creative Network where I first got a chance to perform this play as a monologue which set the wheels in motion to where we are today. Matt Maltby, Nick Oliver, and their work for Pint-Sized, who were the first to believe in the play and my voice and really allowed me to view myself as a writer.

Robert Awosusi and Simeon Blake-Hall for bringing a short extract of it to life with joy and detail, I'll never forget the first time I got to see *Bullring* in front of an audience. Wildcard Theatre and Andy Twyman, unfortunately due to COVID we never got a chance to really start our journey, however the time and free space I was offered in their HQ was invaluable!

Free Hand Scripts for offering free dramaturgical support, for writers who are new their work is so vital. Anna Himali Howard who was my dramaturg and offered thoughtful, detailed feedback and those notes were the springboard to me entering the Bruntwood Prize.

Luke Wilson for the amazing performance at the Prize and beautiful openness and generosity working through our R&D. My friends from back home in all my different group chats also Adaya Henry who initially empowered me to write. Alice Finn for keeping me sane, levelheaded, and being my own secret in-house dramaturg, copywriter, and editor.

Rebecca Need-Menear for the amazing artwork and Manwah Siu and Mrin Roy for standing in the most awkward of positions to elegantly throw roses around me. Tom Finn from Regular Practice for his skill, detail and care in creating the typeface.

My brilliant acting agents at Denton Brierley, Suzy & Sabrina for their support and understanding and my wonderful writing agents at Curtis Brown, Camilla and Katie, for their guidance and care as I've navigated this exciting new journey of my career. The Unicorn Theatre and Theatre Deli for being spaces that are more than just my part time jobs.

Dermot for his amazing passion and belief in the piece and all of the creative team for their endless work on the play. The team at Concord Theatricals, the judges and readers from the Bruntwood Prize, Suzanne Bell and the team at the Royal Exchange for their endless support, the whole team at Paines Plough for the opportunity, Corey Campbell and The Belgrade Theatre team for their essential support and Ellie Keel for truly believing in myself, the play, helping us all to realise its potential and working so hard to get us to this amazing moment we find ourselves in.

Finally shout outs to Birmingham, growing up there played a big part in who I am today and if I was from somewhere else there's no way this play is the same play.

0121 to di worldddd

Part One

(Birmingham. Brum. 0121. The Jewellery Quarter. A small underwhelming studio flat. On the walls are family photos and retro Aston Villa posters. Ashley Young and John Carew. IYKYK. As the audience walk in, we see **NATHANIEL***, smug and cheeky. He's getting ready to go out for...something. We are unsure as to what at this moment.)*

(Music playing out of a speaker. [Music from Birmingham.])

NATHANIEL. I get off the phone to my mom and she all like "you're a lovely, handsome, charming young man." Now if that's true...and my mom would never lie to me...and you know...it's true, then I can't be shit at dating because I'm a gift from God enit.

So maybe what my mom is tryna say is I'm not shit at dating just everyone I meet is shit at dating me.

A few people have said that my date history is weird and tragic, by a few I mean the mandem, my dad, the guy in the nightclub toilet who gives me a lollipop when I give him a pound.

Like...listen so I'm on a first date in Bella Italia with LeToya who said she likes Disney, now I don't love Disney like that so I'm thinking outside of the box. So, when she goes for a bite of her spaghetti bolognaise and I meet her at the other end of her piece of spaghetti to recreate that scene from the *Lady and the Tramp*, that is not weird and tragic. That is wholesome. That is romantic.

It is weird and tragic however to draw attention to us in the restaurant by screaming "OH MY GOD WHAT'RE YOU DOING YOU WEIRDO" then watch as I'm escorted out of the restaurant and banned from Bella Italias for life! Who even goes to Bella Italia anymo-

Anyway...today is a new day and I have a new date! There is nothing quite like getting back on the dating scene after a two-week sabbatical. I love everything about first dates...meeting a new person, getting to know more about them, the first time you touch, the eye contact, do you go for the first kiss or do you not...

(Awkward silence.)

The awkward silences.

I'm not picky either I just want someone like me, a nice personality, a good sense of humour and nice elbows.

I met her on a dating app and on her profile, it says "I'M THE BEYONCÉ OF KINGSTANDING" so I was smooth with it and said could I be the Jay-Z to your Beyoncé, HOV!

You know minus the whole cheating thing, fighting the sister in the lift thing and obviously I'm 100 times more handsome than Jay-Z we ain't got the same lip situation, you know his lips come like this?

To be 100% with you this girl seems like she could be the ONE, and hold on a second, let me land, I'm not being crazy, I've been through this process A LOT. I think there's a genuine potential for love...and I don't mean that getting married shit or "Oooh we went around the canals of Venice" relationship stint. There are more canals in Birmingham than Venice!

I'm talking real love, I'm talking 90s RnB music video outside in the rain kind of love. I'm saying in ten years' time we're having a massive argument in IKEA because she wants the Pysslingar but I want the Kryddnejlika and we can't afford both because the government have set up our society so that our generation are constantly struggling. You know that kind of love.

I'm meeting up with her tonight for the first time, I'm gonna treat her so nice, she deserves the world. Honestly, I feel truly privileged, nay, blessed to be in her presence, let alone be able to speak to her...wow, she really is Beyoncé.

So, I've got a full plan in place for tonight...but before I even consider meeting Beyoncé later, I have a very important meeting.

You see in life there is only one person who's always there for you, nurtures you through some of the toughest times in your life, someone who is always there to talk to about anything and will always make you feel your absolute best.

(Beat.)

That's why a man's relationship with his barber is one of the most sacred relationships on earth.

You see this trim?

You see the detail?

You see the TLC put into this trim?!

I love no person on this earth more than my barber and I ain't afraid to say that. We go through our ups and downs, but he is always there... Apart from today, the most important day of my life, when he goes on holiday, now barbers don't go on holidays often they've got a business to run but when they do its back to the Caribbean for eighteen weeks!

Why can't they just do up like an old white lady?

Ooh long weekend getaway to Benidorm with Frank.

A long weekend is three, maybe four days. Eighteen weeks is 126 days. That's officially four months pregnant. A whole child could be brewing inside of me.

I get a trim once every two weeks that means I'm missing nine trims and I can't not get a trim, I'm not a monster.

So that means I have to go to a new barber...do you know how dirty I feel just sleeping around with next man all willy nilly? My head belongs to my barber and when he's giving me a trim? I sit back and close my eyes and let him do his artistry. It's like our mind, bodies and soul intertwine and our chakras align with one another and we are one.

So, I urgently need a trim, and on a Saturday it's mythlehem tryna get a booking and nearby there's only really the three wise men in terms of barbers whilst mine is away.

Number One. **Hand Of God Barbers**

So, pros and cons. A con is everyone in there looks like their favourite pet has just died, sad. Another con is it smells like jollof rice. Don't get me wrong jollof rice is calm, I just don't mix it with my follicles. Another con is everyone goes in there clapped and comes out even more clapped. A pro is that they're also a phone shop, so I can get my screen repaired while I'm there, which is cool... I guess. There aren't really any other pros to be honest.

Number Two. **Turkish Barber & Shisha Lounge**

A pro is they treat you like a king when you're in there, they do the hot towel and that, they light that ball on a stick thing on fire that burns the hairs in your ear, the shop is presentable, and all types of ethnicities go in there so they're a versatile people. A con? Fuck me do they love to talk, I talk to my barber but he's been cutting my hair for years! We had to crawl before we could walk and walk before we could run. These man are here asking me about where I shop. You don't go on a first date and full on kiss the person before saying hello do you? That first kiss is the moment. It solidifies everything. Some people literally have zero social awareness and even when the convo dies down it's like they have to resuscitate it. Let it rest in peace my guy!

My third and final option. **Renegade Gentlemen's Club**

I know it sounds a bit like a strip club but actually the strip club is next door. So yeah, the more you know. Pros about this place it's clean, nice, kinda boujee and I'm a boujee guy. They also have pictures of famous brummies they've done over the years, the guy who set up Gymshark, Joe Lycett and Jack Grealish. A con is I look nothing like them man, they probably would look at my 'fro and try to approach it with scissors and I'm not paying £50 excluding VAT for a haircut.

I guess it's the Turkish barbers then, I just won't brush my teeth and hopefully they'll not want me to talk back to them.

Google Maps says it's a fifteen-minute walk which is the other side of town so that's a calm walk for a Saturday. As I'm about to leave I get a message from the group chat

(Phone notification buzzer.)

GROUP CHAT MEMBER 1. What you man on

GROUP CHAT MEMBER 3. Nothing still uno

GROUP CHAT MEMBER 4. Mmm man are just ouchea

GROUP CHAT MEMBER 2. I hear dat uno

NATHANIEL. *(Aside.)* What was anyone gaining from that interaction?

Yo, you man I'm about to get a trim at this barbers and I'm a bit uncertain. I've got a date and I don't want to get wigged.

GROUP CHAT MEMBER 3. You linking another girl again?!

NATHANIEL. Don't watch that.

GROUP CHAT MEMBER 1. Yo why don't you try out Shape Upz Barbers?

GROUP CHAT MEMBER 4. Mmm I went with them the other day did me up quick still and they do some celebs and footballers and dat

GROUP CHAT MEMBER 2. I hear dat uno fam

NATHANIEL. I get the link and I see they're based on Instagram and the only way to book an appointment is through Instagram DMs. I've never really slid in another man's DMs before, especially behind my main barber's back, doesn't feel right.

> *(Phone notification buzzer.)*

yo what's good bro, I'm looking to get a trim for later tonight.

BARBER. Yeah bruddah I just had a cancellation so I can see you in 15 minutes if you can make it

> *(*Flame emoji*.)*

> *(*Praising hands emoji*.)*

> *(*Flame emoji*.)*

NATHANIEL. *(Aside.)* Bare emojis and that. Okay...

Yeah bro that's calm I'll see you there. Ermmm

> *(*Fist emoji?*.)*

BARBER. Yes fam! You're about to get the sharpest trim from the best barber in the 0121

> *(*Barber pole emoji*.)*

I've done some of the most high profile people in this country fam

(*100 emoji*.)

This is about to be a movie bro

(*Praising hands emoji*.)

(*Fist emoji*.)

(*Collision emoji*.)

(*Flame emoji*.)

drip will be real my g

(*Water emoji*.)

(*Water emoji*.)

(*Water emoji*.)

see you in a hot sec bro

(*Kissing face emoji*.)

...

That last emoji was an accident my g, it was in my recently used. Sorry.

(*Frown emoji*.)

NATHANIEL. I walk into the city centre; I live in a studio flat in the jewellery quarter so kinda gentrified but it's a part of the city dedicated to jewellery, so it was already gentrified before gentrification was a word.

I reach the barbers. My heart is pounding fast, why am I so nervous? It can't be because of Beyoncé, I guess I've never really done "It" this blatantly with another man before especially one who's sending me kissy face emojis.

We lock eyes, I give him a firms and he gestures at me to sit down, he's dressed in chef whites...including the hat, has a head lamp as if he's mining or reading in the dark and a badge that says "Follicle Engineering Technician."

Asks me if I want anything to drink. *(Kisses teeth.)* Tryna be all smooth and that... I say yeah 'cause my mouth's dry.

The barber cape goes over me and it's clipped on. I'm in it now, there is no turning back, I'm a faithful young black man and here I am sitting in another man's chair. This new breddah knows I'm doing something dirty as well, this hairline isn't his piece of work, I'm not his Mona Lisa. He knows how important this trim is for the both of us, he could have a new customer, I could have a new man... I mean barber, I could have a new barber.

The décor is rah nice, they've got some Donald Rodney artwork and old pictures of Birmingham taken by Vanley Burke. I think I see my dad in one of the pictures but then I see other customers who are obviously regulars here staring at me and I know what they're thinking, you sket. In this day and age, I'm getting slutshamed, sad.

Before we begin, he asks if he can take a before picture for his Instagram page. Now I'm a progressive and forward-thinking person but Rule 101 in life, you can never be seen on your sideting's Instagram! And it's always the sidetings that wanna post you on there. I politely decline whilst covering my face "Ah nah fam I'm not really trying to go public like that, just like to keep a low profile." He's cool and turns on his clippers.

I just try and close my eyes think about my date with Beyoncé and let him proceed with his workmanship, but how am I meant to relax when some stranger is gripsing up my head top, with his slimy E.T. fingers.

A couple minutes pass and it's seemingly going okay. He's faced me away from the mirror, smart I can't critique his every move this way.

He puts down the clippers and brings up the smaller one with the sharper buzzing sound, like a bee on helium, I don't know the name of them, but I know this means he's about to start the shape up. The most integral part to any haircut, this is where the barber earns their dough, throughout this whole time we haven't even spoke one word.

Silence.

You could cut the tension with a razor blade.

He's tapped the clipper into some baby powder and shaped up the main front of my hairline, and now he's hitting the vertical line on one of my corners.

(*Beat.*)

That's when I notice the noise of the clipper closer to my ear than I've ever heard it before.

Then I feel a sudden breeze that I've never experienced on the side of my head.

It clicked... This dickhead went back on my hairline. I freak out, can't breathe, panic attack.

"WHAT HAVE YOU DONE I'M SEEING BEYONCÉ TODAY AND YOU'VE GONE BACK ON MY HAIRLINE."

I run out the barber's chair and run straight back to my apartment... That's why the cape is in my house in case anyone was wondering.

Thing is with a new barber sometimes you don't click it's like when you meet one of your parents' friends for the first time in a few years and you don't have a clue who they are and they're like "Wow I haven't see you since you were this big" and you give them the no teeth smile.

(Phone notification buzzer.)

BARBER. Yo my bro I'm sorry it ended like that

(*Frown emoji*.)

That's not how the Birmingham Mail's barber of the year likes his clientele to feel

(*Fist emoji*.)

Next time I swear I'll nice you up my g free of charge.

I didn't realise you were part of the Beyhive

(*Bee emoji*.)

(*Black heart emoji*.)

NATHANIEL. Some man use the black heart emoji 'cause for whatever reason it's a harder kind of man love, whereas if it was a red heart I'd suddenly assume that he wanted to marry me...

I mean I use it sometimes, when you don't know what to say but you wanna show the mandem you care, it's useful.

Love is love, we all need it.

(Beat.)

I get the rest of my hairline resurrected at the Turkish barbers but now time is of the essence. Get my head back in the game as I get ready for the most important date of my life.

Big rule with me, no two dates are the same 'cause no two people are the same. A bespoke service and I've got the whole evening mapped out.

First, we meet...maybe a lil hug kinda greeting and I'll try and hold it for around three or four Mississippis 'cause I don't want to seem too keen.

Then she might compliment my shirt 'cause it's a nice shirt and everyone always does, then she may say I smell wonderful because I always use great aftershave.

Then my skin? Glowing. Complexion is freeeeesshhhh... I did have a bath with this bath bomb I got from Lush, and it smells amazing but it's given my skin this shimmery shine because I think it had glitter in it. I hope she doesn't notice that.

Some people like to go for food but after Bella Italia I'm not really tryna be caught in any restaurant 'cause you know they all chat to each other.

There's a bar that has loads of board games and things like ping pong, pool, mini arcade section. She said she likes to drink cocktails, she's competitive but also wants to be able talk so it's perfect for the gaming competitive aspect but also not like a nightclub bar so we can still hear each other properly. The cocktails are meant to be the best around. It's the perfect spot.

We initially connected over our love of rum so provided things go well after the gaming bar I know this sick underground rum bar with rums from all over the world.

That's so in her head she's like "this is so nice I love this gaming bar" then I'm like BLAOW! Hit her with the even nicer.

Then hopefully she's feeling like "wow this is really nice I've enjoyed my time" and I'll say, "I've had a good time maybe we should call it a night, until next time?"

I don't even want to reveal too much 'cause a couple people here will start teefing man's methods.

(To the audience.) Like you fam, I see you.

(Whispers.) So most people nowadays will be winning on a date and then push their luck a bit too far. "ah babes you should come mine you know" I go hard down the gentleman route I'll take her to her taxi and

drop a calm peck on the cheek and say "I had a lovely evening and if you like hopefully I can see you again."

You see a first kiss, that is the moment, it's special.

You can't rush it; you'll know when it's time. The moment your lips touch something inside of you changes. All the dots just connect, and everything comes together and makes sense. Your endorphins interweave and you're bonded. It's spiritual but it's otherworldly.

    (Beat.)

That's how you treat a person on a first date, open, honest, show a small form of affection and give reassurance. None of this waiting for a message shit.

You know what, I might write a book or make this my job. You know like that Will Smith film *Hitch*. Big man ting, I can be that but from Birmingham.

Yeahhhh, Hitch, Birmingham, Birmingham, Hitch, the Birmingham Hitch... The Bitch.

    (Beat.)

Sorry!

I'm meeting her at 7:00 p.m. and its 6:30 p.m. and it'll take like twenty minutes to get there, and you can't be late to a first date.

Would you be late to a job interview? They're literally the same thing just a successful job interview gives you money, weird social events like Thirsty Thursdays and if you work for one of those big companies that run everything you might get free cocaine.

A successful date gives you love enit? if you're dating a dealer, you might get free cocaine too.

    (Phone notification buzzer.)

BEYONCÉ. Hi Nathaniel, I'm super sorry but somethings come up and I don't think I can make it tonight!

NATHANIEL. Oh swear, that's fine. I hope everything's okay with you, would you like to rearrange for tomorrow or another time I can still change the booking? (*Smile face emoji*.) kiss.

BEYONCÉ.

(*Beat.*)

NATHANIEL. She left me on read? Sick.

Just switch up out of nowhere, we've been talking for a month, I took it slow, learned from my mistakes, did everything right then I just get taken for a dickhead again? No one forced her to talk to me for a month why does it all switch up now?

Proper thought we were gonna be Birmingham's answer to Beyoncé and Jay-Z...

(**NATHANIEL** *sings a bit of the chorus from "'03 Bonnie & Clyde" by Jay-Z.*)

I went to a serial killer of a barber for no reason, wearing my nice shirt, with glitter all up in my pores.

You know what, it doesn't even matter got to keep it moving. I can save my money, a night in for one.

Get a takeaway, might even do a facemask or something just because I ain't gotta impress anyone doesn't mean I can't look after myself ya zi mi.

I'm a nice guy, I just want someone to be nice with.

(*Beat.*)

(*Kisses teeth.*)

I swear someone playing with your heart is like an extreme form of terrorism.

Part Two

(Four days later.)

NATHANIEL. Yooo what's good? Been a coupla days, just getting on with everyday life but we are fast approaching the weekend and bwoy I cannot wait.

I work in a call centre Monday–Friday making calls and occasionally receiving calls but it's mainly outbound, I hate it and it's soul destroying, but after my master's I moved back home for one month.

It's weird moving back home after Uni, 'cause you're this independent adult, then you go back to living with your "family" the people society tells you you're supposed to love, but you can't stand them for more than three hours at a push let's be real. Bearing in mind the last time you spent this much time with them you were seventeen.

I love my Mom but she's sometimes a bit too...inna, you know what I mean? I don't want to be constantly mothered unless it's on my say so.

Is that selfish?

Family is tough to navigate. Mainly my dad, born and raised in Spanish town, Jamaica and moved here when he was a teenager.

He's a rock with a wealth of knowledge who's always there for me and simultaneously my sworn enemy.

My Dad thinks I'm too British, he hates how British I've become even though he decided to raise me in Britain. As far as he's concerned there is no difference between me and Mary Berry.

He hates British things I do, like when I say sorry for no specific reason, he always says *"bwoy you say sorry one more time then I'll give you something to be sorry about"*

I don't even bother speaking to him on a level or I get the:

"Dis ah big people talk"

"Oh you tink seh you big now?"

I think I've grown as a person and you're meant to move out after Uni, collect your degree, get that grad job where you can progress through the ranks and then be financially stable by the time you're thirty.

I'd say I'm on track, it might not be the right track but we're still moving.

I studied Fine Art, so jobs are far and few between, which is what my Careers Advisor warned me about at college and I bet you she's still in her tiny little office, sipping her black coffee from the shitty Kenco machine that's been there since the 90s with her one sweetener in it all smug.

(Kisses teeth.)

I proper thought I was gonna be a hybrid, edgy, sexy kind of Brum town Basquiat with a garnish of Banksy and the national treasure potential of David Hockney.

I rah love what I do you know, it's just hard to stay motivated when it feels like you've done everything you're meant to, played the game, learned from mistakes and everything around you is made for you, but you don't quite fit in so I'm just "other." You know what I mean?

Kinda like I'm a pink lady apple from the rag market but I'm being sold in the organic section at Whole Foods. You all know the market apple is the better apple so why is everyone buying the shitty organic one?

Anyways when I make enough money I'll start to focus full time, just gotta balance,

Rent

Bills

Food

Student loan

Social life

Inflation

and I'm bless.

So, it's a dead-end job till I find something that fuels my creativity or my crippling crippling debt. Which is fine, this job means I can live by myself and attempt to enjoy my life somehow?

I mean I love art, it's what makes me truly happy, my reason to be, my raison d'être if you will, it's the fabric of culture, it lives on way beyond our lifetimes, to create something bigger than yourself? The purest expression of the human mind, that fills my spirit with excitement and optimism...

I haven't done a single thing since starting this job. It's hard to pursue your passion when you're a cog in the machine of capitalism but it's harder to get out of the machine.

(Beat.)

I dunno.

At work we get cool incentives and bonuses for people who can sign up the most clients in a week. I can happily announce to you all I am your reigning champion for the third week in a row. You're welcome. The champ is here.

(Shows wrestling belt.)

We don't actually get a wrestling belt, but it makes things more interesting when you walk into meetings with a belt over your shoulder.

One of the down parts is how shit my office chair is. It's on wheels but doesn't swivel, what kind of caveman developed this sort of chair.

Me and the mensdem have previously discussed these issues in forensic detail. See here from a few years ago...

> *(Phone notification buzzer.)*

GROUP CHAT MEMBER 1. Yoooo mandem big news.

GROUP CHAT MEMBER 4. rrrrrrrrr swear down.

NATHANIEL. What is it?

GROUP CHAT MEMBER 1. Peep my new work chair.

GROUP CHAT MEMBER 3. naaaaaaa that's mad

GROUP CHAT MEMBER 4. That looks harddddd bro congrats n dat

GROUP CHAT MEMBER 2. I appreciate the curvature that will hopefully support the issues in your lower lumbar region coupled with the fact it is very fashionable, height and width adjustable that's a shrewd purchase from your offices you must be a very valued member. I'm proud of you my bro.

NATHANIEL. This was how he spoke before he started smoking weed everyday now, he just says shit like "I hear dat uno" and...that's it to be honest.

I don't get why he started smoking it so much. It was probably whe–

I hear my manager coming!

I don't put my phone away because I'm scared he'll shout at me; I put it away because if I look busy, he won't talk to me.

He's probably in my top three people I wouldn't wanna be stuck in a long conversation with...

Third Place

Anyone who potentially wants to make a podcast, 'cause once you're five minutes deep into conversation they say *"yo we should make a podcast"* I don't wanna make a podcast.

Second Place

Noel Edmonds. Why is he so smug? Why does he always have a certain lightness to his step. What does he know that we don't? apart from who the banker really is?

First Place

My manager, the best way to describe him is... Imagine a blind black guy born in the southern states of America hearing nothing but racism his whole life but doesn't realise it's directed at him so he thinks it's the norm. Except he's English, he's not blind and he's from east London so basically my manager is a racist black guy with a cockney accent.

I knew he was slightly tapped when he offered me the job then pulled me close and said, "I don't want any of your Mandems outside the office at 5:00 p.m. alright."

Mandems. Mandems?

A sure tell sign that someone is an undercover cop is when they add that S to the end of Mandem. Mandem is already a group of people. So, what is the S for? The S at the end stands for shtupid.

He comes over with his usual spiel of asking if I met up with any of my *"Mand*ems" if I brought any of that *"proper ethnic"* food because once I brought in curry goat, rice and peas. Which sounds fine, but actually as a black person bringing home cooked food into an office environment is like an extreme sport.

It's an adrenaline rush, 'cause once white people get a whiff of your food like my dad would say *"dem come like darg."* Start putting their beaks in your food and you hear shit like

"corrr that smells good"

"oh my god what the fuck is that smell"

"ooooh my nose is burning can spicy travel through the air"

Can spicy travel through the air? I don't know are you a dickhead??? I just do Tesco meal deals now.

One of the best parts of the day is when I go to get coffee but actually it's just time where I chat shit about other people. I usually meet my boy, mi amigo, my sidekick, The bull to my ring, the Robin to my Batman.

When I say he's my boy I mean Monday–Friday, 9–5, I love that man, I'd kill for my guy, my number one bredrin, My Best Friend. Outside of that, I don't actually know anything about him, but he seems cool, we have a secret code so we know when it's time, it's like an office version of the bat signal basically he does this. (**NATHANIEL** *shows us the secret sign.*)

Today I saw Robin, and he was smiling from ear to ear. I haven't told anyone at work about how Beyoncé did me dirty but for some reason everything he says to me reminds me of her.

(**ROBIN***'s responses are in the style of Beyoncé.*)

Robin! Coffee!

ROBIN. *Heeeeeeey*

NATHANIEL. What's good bro

ROBIN. *Listen*

NATHANIEL. ...ok how was your weekend?

ROBIN. *I've been alone when I'm surrounded by friends how could the silence be so loud*

NATHANIEL. Yeah man I hear that you know... I got stood up on a date this weekend pretty rough to be honest but I'm gonna try and get in touch again maybe. I dunno.

ROBIN. *I'll be damned if I see another chick on your arm*

NATHANIEL. ...why?

ROBIN. *You don't know how impressing your curiosity was*

NATHANIEL. To who???

ROBIN. *Kelly and Michelle*

NATHANIEL. Both Kelly and Michelle like me?! Michelle is the one in HR enit but I haven't spoken to Kelly is she accounting?

ROBIN. *To the left to the left*

NATHANIEL. Ohhhhhhh Marketing! Should I ask one of them out?

ROBIN. *Yes*

NATHANIEL. I dunno man with the wrestling belt and stuff I always thought people around here hate me and think I do too much.

ROBIN. *Some call it Arrogant, I call it confident*

NATHANIEL. Thanks bro I appreciate you man I just need to portray that confidence and ask one of them out enit.

ROBIN. *Can't you see there's no other man above you?*

NATHANIEL. You're right! You really think I should go for it enit?

ROBIN. *All I can say is yes, yes, yes, all I can say is, yes yes yes yes.*

NATHANIEL. ...ok thanks mate

ROBIN. *How we smart enough to make these millions, Strong enough to bear the children, Then get back to business*

NATHANIEL. I mean it's an average salary call centre but yeah let's get back to work.

So, two girls are interested in moi???

You talk in French when you talk about love.

I would be shocked, but you know how they say to play Mozart when you're in the womb to make you intelligent? When my mom was six months pregnant, she went to a Boyz 2 Men concert and Luther Vandross so it's the same concept but amplified for where I get at least 90% of my sex appeal from.

Now I can't date two girls that work in the same office at the same time…in this economic climate?! I know fuck all about either of them, they work on the other side of the office which is the equivalent of the north and south divide.

So, it's time for the big guns… The nuh bodda wid yuh chupidness check formally known as the Don't Be Stupid check.

The Don't Be Stupid Check is a personal background check where I can find out whether they're right for me and I'm right for them and all of their previous history also known as a DBS.

Everyone does it with potential partners. However, you can't do it alone the workload is too much, and your opinion is biased as you may already have a favourite.

That's where the group chat comes in.

(Phone notification buzzer.)

Yo mandem, two girls at work are into me and I can only date one.

GROUP CHAT MEMBER 4. Who says you can't date two

(*Devil smiling emoji*.)

NATHANIEL. Lowe it man, I have respect unlike you.

GROUP CHAT MEMBER 4. I'm playing just send the details over.

NATHANIEL. Aite their names are Michelle and Kelly, and they work at the same place as me

GROUP CHAT MEMBER 1. Yeah, yeah, we're all on it asap

(*Handshake emoji*.)

GROUP CHAT MEMBER 3. Yeah, Nath we got this bro

GROUP CHAT MEMBER 2. I hear dat uno

NATHANIEL. You see this, working together for the greater good? It's like when the avengers assemble.

The operation is thorough but foolproof, a full team working night and day collecting data from various avenues such as mutual friends, previous people they've dated, Instagram, Facebook, using burner accounts. It's like when the British army cracked the German Enigma code.

(Phone notification buzzer.)

GROUP CHAT MEMBER 1. Done check your fax machine.

NATHANIEL. See! That was done expeditiously, I'm positive me and the lads could have a Private Investigator Firm where we all wear long coats and talk weird.

Ok so Michelle is a health and fitness guru on Instagram who spends a lot of time in London. She's from Brighton, but she went to Uni in Brum and stuck around.

She studied psychology...bit of a red flag, I don't need a therapist.

She has a sausage dog called Prosperity who also has an Instagram account where it's all in first person, and she's previously referred to herself as an influencer.

Her world appears to be crushed grey velvet and her mom and dad have Tory potential.

Oh and her last "soulmate" was one of those white guys who lives in rural Thailand with dreads.

Kelly is actually private on all forms of social media so she was a harder cookie to crack. Obviously we cracked it though, that's the magic of the game.

She studied art like me, she is also from Birmingham. She grew up in Great Barr but lives in a place called Solihull so not Birmingham.

If that posh family from Gogglebox were from Birmingham, they'd live in Solihull.

People from Solihull say to people outside of Birmingham that they're from Birmingham 'cause no one knows where Solihull is but actually people from Solihull sometimes are really precious about the fact they are from Solihull and not Birmingham.

It's a pride thing but also mildly classist. Midlands Politics, very thorough.

Her parents are from Handsworth though which is where my parents lived when they were younger before moving to Erdington.

Her mom works at my old primary school and her dad is a university lecturer. Her insta is very understated, doesn't post often the occasional travel picture or a picture of her at a family function.

That's it, I kinda like the mystery there is more to find out. Let's do a vote hands up for Michelle?

(*Invites the audience.*)

Hands up for Kelly?

(*Invites the audience.*)

Why?

(*Unplanned audience interaction end up going with* **KELLY** *no matter what.*)

(*Phone notification buzzer.*)

Hi Kelly, I spoke to Robin and was wondering if you'd like to go on a date? Kiss

(*Aside.*) Now in my years of texting I'm probably gonna be waiting a while for a repl...

KELLY. Hey Nathaniel, I'd love to! Meet around 7:30 pm? Kiss Kiss

NATHANIEL. Sure! What would you like to do? Kiss Kiss Kiss

KELLY. I've got the whole evening planned out if that's okay with you? Kiss Kiss Kiss Kiss

NATHANIEL. Wow the script has turned, the tables flipped. No like wow it's like I'm going on a date with me and I'm fucking catch and to think some of you wanted me to date Michelle?!

(*Picks audience member.*)

Yeah I'm tutting and shaking my head at you. Oh, shit erm play it cool

errrrrrm. Ah cool beans sounds wicked. I can't wait!

No no no no no.

Yeah, sounds good, I look forward to your plans...

Who always plans stuff?

I look forward to your plans Jennifer Lopez

KELLY. What do you mean haha

NATHANIEL. Ah fuck, that *"haha"* is severe uncertainty on the reference.

Jennifer Lopez plays a wedding planner in the film wedding planner. Sorry, shit joke.

KELLY. Oh, talking about marriage already, are you? well I hope your prepared to meet your monster in law!

NATHANIEL. Nice she hit back at my joke with a better joke she's funnier than me. WAIT! She's funnier than me??????

Part Three

NATHANIEL. Friday night.

Date night.

Excitement and nerves but not like butterflies, more like you know when you have loads of layers on and you take one of them off, but it rides up over your head and then you're trapped inside a T-Shirt and a Jumper and have a mini heart attack because you fear you will never see the light of day ever again??

It's like that feeling, so not too bad.

At Uni I always referred to my three tension states.

Tension State One – Sitting down to piss

You're tired, stressed, can't be arsed to stand up and fight. You need to take a break. You sit down. Honestly men need to normalise this anyway.

Tension State Two – Straddling the toilet to piss

It looks like this; this is down in the dumps man. This stress possesses your soul, you may recognise this seating position if your PE teacher ever had to teach music classes or when some random people came into school to do assembly and they wanted to relate to the youth. I haven't done this since Farrah left me.

> *(Beat.)*

Sometimes I'd bring a pillow and just rest my head on the tank lid.

Tension State Three – Pissing your pants

The stress hits out of nowhere and there you are pissing your pants. Self-explanatory honestly. Rock bottom, you don't even care.

Right now, I'm between One and Two, mainly because I don't have any idea where I'm going or what I'm doing all I know is we're meeting at 7:30 p.m. at the Town Hall.

I respect it though if you ever date someone the place you meet says a lot about them.

Like if they said meet outside the Bull at the Bullring or the Maccies on the ramp I'd say they're childish and be worried about their true intentions.

However, the Town Hall is an inspired choice. The Greek architecture, the location it just screams magnifique.

As I'm walking up, I see her standing outside and she looks beautiful, like trust me I've gone on a lot of dates but immediately this feels different, it's not just a physical beauty I can sense it, you can feel the aura surrounding her, it's kind of indescribable...it's so enticing.

I'm close to Tension State Three but then she turns around sees me and smiles and immediately everything feels okay.

We hug and listen yeah; I thought I might've been the best hugger in the Midlands at least top ten but mate... she's better. She smells like a successful independent perfume shop.

She says we're going to this bar she thinks I might like but is keeping it a secret. Before we set off towards New Street, she has a surprise for me...pulls out a miniature bottle of rum.

"Just to take the edge off" she says.

I can't believe I've never thought of that! Really thoughtful, and such a good idea, unless she's trying to poison me.

As we're walking, we see some Birmingham City football fans going into New Street station. She says she hates the blues and I'm like holy shit! Till she ruins it and says...

"We're all wolves ay we"

A Wolverhampton Wanderers fan???

> *(Kisses teeth.)*

I knew it was too good to be true, I hide my minor disappointment 'cause I'm never gonna let football get in the way of love. I've seen *Bend It Like Beckham*.

We get outside and it's the underground rum bar, my spot you know! As we arrive, we're greeted by a member of staff who says,

"Oh it's you again I didn't see your name on the reservation list, did you book 'cause we're full tonight?"

I give him the shut the fuck up eyes you know the one. He's completely blind to it though. Kelly says it's booked in her name and he goes to me

"Wow normally you're always the booker"

my man takes us to the table and doesn't shut up

"Yeah you didn't show up for your booking last week did you, our loyal customer, if we did a black card you'd be the first to receive it"

Pure violation.

"We actually have a guessing game of how many different people you will bring here in a month"

Kelly hears all this; it's embarrassing and just mean.

> *(Beat.)*

When you become a...serial dater like...I guess I am. There are spots you will prefer more than others, almost like a safe space. Your face does become familiar, and I've never really considered that the staff will notice and then use it for their own amusement.

"Suh it guh" as my Dad would say.

(To **KELLY***.)* I'm sorry Kelly, I go on a lot of dates tryna find a person to fill that relationship sized gap in my life.

> *(Beat.)*

This is also one of my favourite bars, I'm sorry, I hope that doesn't put you off I think you're really nice.

KELLY. Its fine, I get it, I'm the exact same I'm a bit of a "serial dater" too but…I think you're really nice…let's do a game of truths just to get to know each other better?

NATHANIEL. She's really nice… We're really nice.

Also, I'm good at truths because I know the exact questions to find out all I need, and it's not would you rather watch your parents have sex every night for the rest of your life or join in once to make It stop. It's the real shit.

Our drinks arrive, she orders a cocktail called *"Good things Rum to those who wait"* I just got a rum old fashioned, we cheers and thankfully she didn't ask to boomerang it and I start.

What's your favourite animated film released between 2000–2006?

(Aside.) It may feel weird and specific but trust me.

KELLY. *Shrek.*

> *(Squeal of excitement from* **NATHANIEL** *to the audience.)*

What's your biggest pet peeve?

NATHANIEL. People who call themselves a night owl when owls tend to be nocturnal. You're just an Owl. You're Hedwig. You?

KELLY. The fact a dishwasher is a dish washer, but the washing Machine is THE Washing Machine.

NATHANIEL. Mmmmm! Irrational Fear?

KELLY. People who put socks on before they put on their underwear... you don't do that do you?

NATHANIEL. No, I'm not a threat to society.

KELLY. Good. You?

NATHANIEL. Irrational Fear... Oh, I have this recurring nightmare about Men in turtlenecks performing spoken word poetry.

　　　(Nervous silence.)

KELLY. LITERALLY WHY DO THEY TALK LIKE THAT!

NATHANIEL. MY POINT EXACTLY! *(Aside.)* We get some shots.

KELLY. Favourite fruit?

NATHANIEL. Guinep... you?

KELLY. Oh! I call those Chenets, I'd say mine are probably Strawberries.

NATHANIEL. *(Aside.)* Strawberries are such a fruit of circumstance you can have a strawberry and it tastes like a wet cloth but there's a nice two-week period once a year where it tastes great, and it means it gets treated like royalty for doing the bare minimum for the other fifty weeks of the year. If a strawberry is your favourite fruit you have to take a long hard look at yourself and realise, you're a prisoner of the moment.

Ah strong choice! Least favourite alcoholic drink?

KELLY. Lager or Beer… they all taste the same just some are cheaper than others you?

NATHANIEL. Pink Moscato… what's the point. I may as well drink pink lemonade.

(Aside.) We grab another round.

Your own profound statement or opinion?

KELLY. The water that hardens the egg softens the potato… you?

NATHANIEL. I think pillows are indicative of white privilege.

KELLY. What's gives you your purpose in life? Like your Raison d'être?

> *(Beat.)*

NATHANIEL. I dunno…stuff enit.

KELLY. Yeah, but it's something! Come on you're so specific about everything but not what gives you purpose? Like what gets you out of bed in the morning? For me I've made enough money from the job to move into the education sector, I start in September. I want to focus on effective alternative teaching methods. Too many young people get put in a box early on in their lives. We're all human, we just need nurturing, time and understanding.

NATHANIEL. Yeah…

(Aside.) We get another drink.

Congratulations that sounds amazing, you'll be amazing I know it.

KELLY. Thanks! I'm so glad to get out of the call centre, I hate it and it's soul destroying…so what makes you happy then?

> *(Beat.)*

NATHANIEL. Why did you ask Robin to set us up together?

KELLY. We've never really spoke but I see you, speaking to others and roaming around the office, you have this beautiful energy that follows you wherever you go. The office is glum, depressing and dry but as soon as you walk in that all changes, everyone can see it. It's why you're always employee of the week and why you'll be successful in whatever you do. I just wanted a chance to get to know you and I'm glad I did. I think you're really special. I bet you don't care about that stuff though.

NATHANIEL. *(Aside.)* I DO CARE! I'm a care bear.

(Still aside.) That's the nicest thing anyone has ever said to me, she sees me and knows me better than I do. As a rule, I don't kiss on the first date, but this is like everything I've ever wanted...is that childish?

KELLY. So yeah, call me childish, but I really like you Nathaniel, you're really sweet. Anyway, last question... what's your musical guilty pleasure?

NATHANIEL. *(Aside.)* We take a shot.

You're gonna think it's weird but...Techno...

KELLY. FUCK OFF I LOVE TECHNO!

NATHANIEL. I've never met another person who likes techno that doesn't either base their whole personality around it or is German.

KELLY. I have an idea! Let's get out of here.

NATHANIEL. As the bartender comes with the bill, I go to pay. However, for some reason my card isn't working. Instead of taking me to the side the bartender puts the card machine to his ear like a phone...

BARTENDER. Hello 999, big emergency, do you give out money if someone on a first date doesn't have any ha.

NATHANIEL. Then he realises it's a WiFi problem. The machine is asking for me to swipe card which hasn't happened since Jennifer Lopez was Jenny from the block.

Worst part is it worked meaning I now have to sign the receipt in front of Kelly. It's embarrassing because I made my signature in year four and haven't changed it since.

After the payment debacle I ask her where we're going, usually the date ends now but we're kind of going with the flow which is fun. We jump in a taxi, and she whispers the location to the driver. I love surprises but this is how people die in movies.

We end up in Digbeth which is sort of like the Shoreditch of Birmingham and there's a massive queue, we're going to a rave.

They're playing Electronic, Garage, House and Techno. I don't really go to techno raves because as a black person they don't feel safe.

Even though I love the music and black people literally created the genre, like most genres. It's thought about as a European genre, but it was invented in Detroit by young black Americans who had nothing but old pieces of equipment. They created this beautiful and pure sound and at that point we'd never heard or experienced anything like it before.

Now it's become so whitewashed the idea of me liking it is weird and not just that, I don't feel comfortable to come to these spaces. How do you create one of the greatest worldwide renowned tables and fast forward a few years you don't even have a seat at it. It's not just techno either, Jazz, Country, Rock n Roll, House and everything that stems from it. I can't believe I said it was a guilty pleasure.

(Techno music playing.)

I step in with a confidence. The rave is like everything I've ever imagined, it's the techno portion of the evening and the strobe lights are reflecting off sweaty bodies like moonlight on a lake, we're in a derelict old factory and it's cold outside but inside it's like the middle of summer, it smells like a boxing gym which some people might think is nasty but to me it's kind of perfect.

Kelly and I stand out in our date night attire, but the beautiful thing is it's so euphoric in here no one cares. Ravers are some of the freest people in the world, you could be dressed as an astronaut, and you'd fit in.

Kelly goes to the toilet, and I go to the bar to get some more drinks.

The DJ is dropping banger after banger. The feeling never static, always acousmatic. Across the way you can see a bald guy by himself at least thirty years older than everyone else looks a bit like my dad and he's going in! Darts me a look. Gives me the nod, then carries on dancing.

I've got two shots and two plastic bottles of wine. However, no sign of Kelly... She's not gonna do me like Beyoncé is she, or LeToya...or Farrah?

> *(Transition into UK garage.)*

Then like that we seamlessly transition into the garage portion of the evening and some gangly, sweaty, white guy wearing sunglasses approaches me...

Goes towards me to as if he's gonna whisper something he leans in, so I lean in...

> *(Beat.)*

Uh oh... I've been in this situation before, Shit, Fuck, Fucking dickhead Nathaniel! As soon as I realise and try to leave it's too late because...

On the Mic I'm way too major

Ganja come straight from Jamaica

Pass me the rizla papers

Smoking some of the finest flavaz

And again

Mic I'm way too major

Ganja from Jamaica

Pass the rizla papers

Smoking on the finest flavaz

This guy, He starts spitting bars right down my flipping ear. I hate it when white people do this, you can't escape.

North, South, East, West

Midlands we do it the best.

0121 big up ya chest

Can't ever give it

Never give it

Wanna have a rest

South, West, North, East

Brum town we're the belly of the beast

Wanna try it with me look down at De-Feat

Wanna try it with Me then I kiss my teeth

Yet here I am kissing my teeth. This is a niche black cultural experience that tends to happen if you're the only black person in a club or a rave full of white people. Which just so happens to be me. I need Kelly but she is nowhere to be seen...

On the mic I'm the controller

Always high I'm never sober.

Blaze up sitting on the sofa.

Give your Mrs the cold shoulder!

I'm killing everything and I'm wearing my sovereign ring.

You'll never win 'cause I'm the king and you'll get dash in the bin.

Man are always billing when I'm spinning,

Ganja smoke up to the ceiling, vibes I'm feeling, rhymes I'm killing. Best at this ting.

See Enemies, send for me, I'm waved off Hennessey, I need some therapy, ganja my remedy.

Every Memory, Cynthia, Beverley, All the girls belling me I need some energy.

Way too cold for Dubai

Way too hot for Finland

Way too cold for July

Hottest Shit in England

Way too cold for Dubai

Way too hot for Finland

Way too cold for July

Hottest Shit in England

All you can do is smile and nod. My dad always says

"Confidence is a feeling of everything unu has experienced in dem lives suh far"

Which begs the question what has this guy gone through to have this level of audacity?

I see Kelly, I give her the eye as if to say If I hear this man say ganja one more time I'll light him on fire like a spliff.

She runs through the crowd with pace and purpose. Like an Olympian, like the Dina Asher-Smith of the Birmingham Rave Scene.

I'm loving life but this is exhausting. There's a certain level of stamina required to be a raver and you don't even have that if you go to the gym every day.

I immediately give Kelly a hug, that was stressful but being in her arms in this weird rave it's like everything in the world and my life is gonna be okay.

I look at her and she looks at me and I'm saying to myself kiss her, this is the moment, this is the person, everything makes sense.

   (Beat.)

Unfortunately, that thought was a bit too long enit? And the moment passes.

Then we just dance the night away to this electronic sound.

My dad was part of a Soundsystem called Acousmatic which means to hear without seeing the source of sound.

So, in that moment you just feel you know what I mean?

Back in the day he used to play with the likes of Steel Pulse and Musical Youth, and he would always jump on the mic once in every set and say...

"The feeling never static, always acousmatic"

And right now, in this sweaty, dusty room with a bunch of musty strangers, with Kelly there's nothing else you can do as the reverb and bass tremors through the airwaves and you're in the moment with someone who makes you feel like you have purpose. All you can do is connect with each other on a deeper level, all you can do is feel.

The rave finishes and its 5:30 a.m., can't even get a kebab or pizza if you wanted. That's how you know you've had a night when it's strictly a taxi home or a Maccies Breakfast.

The sky is starting to go bright, and neither of us want to leave just yet... I know the perfect place to go. My cousin works nights on security at one of the tallest buildings in Birmingham so I drop him a message and he says he can get me in and on the roof.

We get there and you can see the whole city, a full-on panoramic view. Kelly takes my hand; we have a moment and just take in the whole city. I haven't even touched my Maccies hashbrown yet.

If our evening were a Rom Com we would be in the montage where we are doing cute stuff in slow motion, and in the background of you can hear 90s Slow Jamz.

Birmingham gets a lot of shit from people some of who definitely haven't even been or even left their hometown and from up here you can see drunkards fighting, cars racing through the streets, foxes scrummaging through rubbish and that one weird person who likes to go for a run at 6:00 a.m. but underneath those lines of chaos there's a stillness and that's where the real beauty of the City is.

I love my city.

Kelly man, she is magical, If she ate five cloves of raw garlic, I'd still let her breathe in my face.

She can move mountains and planets just with her being. A flower of flowers.

Her coming into my life now is like getting to the end of your packet of Skittles, and you pour your last Skittle into your hand and it's red and you get that feeling you're unstoppable because the red Skittles are the best Skittles.

Yeah man that's her, she's a red Skittle.

I look over to her she gives me the warmest smile and it fills my soul and heart with optimism and excitement, just as I look out again the sun starts to rise.

It's beautiful, the sky has shades of pink, orange and purple, I know what I want to do but I need to stop overthinking it and do it. Just do it. Then she asks me again...

KELLY. What makes you happy?

NATHANIEL. You've made me happy.

Then...

We...

Kiss.

> *(Beat.)*

> *(Beat.)*

> *(Beat.)*

...and there's nothing.

Part Four

(Phone notification buzzer.)

GROUP CHAT MEMBER 4. Bro so what you left a gyal by herself on the roof?

GROUP CHAT MEMBER 1. Nah he said he got her a taxi home. Don't you pay attention.

GROUP CHAT MEMBER 4. Yeah, but more metaphorically enit.

GROUP CHAT MEMBER 2. I hear that uno.

GROUP CHAT MEMBER 3. Moretime though why were you moving like that fam. We've all lipsed a gyal. Maybe she's not feeling you. Just keep it moving.

GROUP CHAT MEMBER 1. Mmm, you had a good night yeah?

GROUP CHAT MEMBER 3. It's been a couple of days. You should go to work. You can't lose your job or you'll end up moving back home.

GROUP CHAT MEMBER 4. You can't say that bro!

GROUP CHAT MEMBER 3. Am I lying though?

GROUP CHAT MEMBER 2. I hear that uno.

GROUP CHAT MEMBER 1. Yeah, bredda just get your head together. We're here if you need anything just remember it ain't that deep *(*Black heart emoji*.)*

NATHANIEL. It rah ain't that deep. I dunno man. Like why I felt like that. Dramatic boy settings. I'm good though. I'll get back to work, money affi mek and life affi live.

GROUP CHAT MEMBER 2. I hear that uno.

NATHANIEL. I'm not going back to work, I'm never gonna go back there.

I handed in my notice, the morning of the rooftop. It's not to avoid Kelly, we're on decent-ish terms. I didn't fully tell her how I felt, what happened.

She was everything, the most beautiful heart and the purest soul.

I don't know how I'll afford to live let alone get back into art I just felt...

    (Beat.)

Everything that's happened in my life led up to that moment and when it happened there was nothing, I saw nothing, I felt nothing, I experienced nothing.

The feeling was...static.

There was just this empty numbness.

I've been reading articles online, reading books. I've seen it say shit like *"existential crisis"* or *"depression."*

    (Beat.)

I've been trying to get in touch with my Dad, I'd usually go to my Mom for things like this but I dunno... I felt like my Dad was... 'cause...what if the feeling isn't acousmatic?

He always says

"as you get older everything start fi hurt"

He's right but it's not a physical pain.

It's a mental strain, the weight of the world and your future and aspirations, everything you want from life suddenly becomes real. Then trying to achieve what you want you get stuck in a shit job that puts you in a maze with no exits.

You're just coasting, till you find the inevitable dead end over and over and over again.

Robin from work has a degree in music you know, Michelle has one in psychology, I work with actors, artists, people with masters' in law and they haven't left the job because they literally don't know how.

The only person who managed to get themselves out into something they love is Kelly. We have so much in common except that one thing.

Then there I am, dating, searching, chasing gyal for a semblance of self.

I'm a regular in these bars and they make fucking fun of me. I have a strategy at how I approach each minor detail and scenario of anything that could happen; that isn't normal.

They say the people you surround yourself with is who you will become, make it sound like it's all down to you but fuck that. It's not my fault, It's not our fault.

That's a societal problem before a people problem, it's Babylon, we're stuck in this system and we have fuck all, we're all human we just need...

    (Beat.)

Nurturing, time and understanding.

I lost any sense of purpose, a raison d'etre before I could even start,

I don't know what makes me happy.

What sort of life is that? What am I even doing here?

How do I find the difference and set the balance between living and just existing?

    (Phone ringing but goes to voicemail.)

Yo whargwarn people Nathaniel here. Well, I'm not here it's a voicemail anyways you should know better than to call me so serves you right... Text, Voicenote,

Phonecall in that order. Leave a message and I'll get back to you though. Love!

DAD. Bwoy you better change ya dyam voicemail about serves me right what a proper English humour. You av to av some sarcastic warra warra voicemail. *(Kisses teeth.)*

I'll let you arf cah you clearly miserable nuh backside.

Lard natty wahum to you son, you is bright, you is smart, you're very talented, and you is funny, when you nuh bodda mek joke like the dyam smug eeeediat Ricky Gervais.

Mi feel sorry fi yu, but at the same time not at all because you're still that same bwoy with alla dem skills and attributes. In the grand scheme of the world yes you aren't successful or the next Citroen Picasso or wah ever him name be, but to me, yuh mudda and the family that surrounds you, we couldn't be prouder.

Everyone have something fi offer to the worl, and I know you have bigger plans than your current job. Listen here bwoy, Move out ya flat, its ugly nuh rass anyways, come back home and get yourself together and back into yuh artistry. I will move all my sound equipment out of the backhouse and that can be yuh room so you have space for yourself to sleep and work. We can't afford much in this life, but to help make our son the success he should be we can afford it all.

You run tings, tings nuh run you.

Alright bwoy call me when you get this. Right? Mmm, mmm, okay, alright. Listen here.

I love you...

End

Milton Keynes UK
Ingram Content Group UK Ltd.
UKHW022055211123
433005UK00014B/675